Critical Praise For GOD'S COUNTRY

Thomas E. Naumann lives with his wife, two sons, and daughter in Union Co, North Carolina. He graduated as a Grayson Scholar from Mars Hill University in the Appalachian Mountains of NC. He is the President and Owner of EatSleepHunt.com and Cherokee Run Hunting Lodge LLC, a guide & outfitting service in Chesterfield, South Carolina. God's Country was inspired by his great passion for the Lord and the outdoors.

"This book will lead anyone to view the outdoors with an enthusiasm that they never had before…you get a clear-cut picture of God's desire for your life."

- Chip Ferguson, Former Quarterback,
Florida State Seminoles

"Tom has captured the essence of what a sportsman sees everyday…showing that everything ties into the Bible and our faith in God."

- Larry Long, 1995 North Carolina Bowhunter of the Year

"In God's Country, Tom presents and paints a vivid picture of exciting encounters with nature…descriptively showing us the beautiful and astounding world that God has created."

- Travis Thompson, Former Pitcher, Cincinnati Reds

GOD'S COUNTRY

A Devotional for the Outdoorsman

Thomas E. Naumann

Published by BookLocker.com, Inc., St. Petersburg, Florida.

Printed on acid-free paper.

BookLocker.com, Inc.
2018

First Edition

Unless otherwise noted, Scripture quotations are taken from the New International Version of the Holy Bible. Copyright 1973, 1978 by the International Bible Society.

Contact the author:
Thomas E. Naumann
P.O. Box 1768
Indian Trail, NC 28079

DEDICATION

Dedicated to my

Lord and Savior Jesus Christ,

My loving wife Angie and beautiful children

Tucker, Tanner, and Tatum

…and Dad for taking me fishing.

Table of Contents

Foreword

Growing up in the North Carolina mountains, I learned early to hunt and fish. Many afternoons, the woods and streams offered welcome refuge from homework, chores and Mama's ever-watchful eye. Along the way, I came to understand that "the earth is the LORD's, and everything in it, the world, and all who live in it" (Psalm 24:1 NIV). I realized that He made not only the outdoors but also me for His glory.

In God's Country, Thomas Naumann reflects on those truths in his own unique way. Down-to-earth and folksy, his insights will help you appreciate more the wonders of God's creation. They'll also bring you face-to-face with the greatest wonder of all - that *"God so loved the world that he gave his one and only Son, that whoever believes in him shall not perish but have eternal life"* (John 3:16 NIV).

May God bless you as you read this enjoyable book.

Franklin Graham

President, Samaritan's Purse

Introduction

"As the deer pants for streams of water, so my soul pants for you O God." Psalm 42:1

For the last few years, the Lord has inspired me to write down what I have learned about Him through my experience as an outdoorsman.

I quickly learned that my passion and zeal for hunting and fishing was greater than it was for God. It is a hard pill to swallow, but one we all need to take. How many of us get more excited for the coming deer season than for church on Sunday? Believe me, I have many a time.

God's Country is a devotional for just about anybody, not just for outdoorsmen. We all marvel at God's Creation from the mountains to the seas. The beauty and purity of wildlife and nature captivate many of us. You don't have to be a sportsman to appreciate what God has created.

It is my hope and prayer for those who read this book, that your life may be touched in a new and special way. Stop, look, and listen to what God may teach you through all that He has created and blessed us with.

Thank you Jesus for coming into my heart as Savior and Lord. As tough as life can be at times, thank you for being my best friend.

God seemed so close in the vast country of South Africa. His Creation is overwhelming!

God's Country - Mountaintop view in the Morganton, NC.

His Creation

If you have ever taken part in any activity in the great outdoors, it is hard to doubt that God created everything you can see. Take a minute and read Genesis 1. From the most beautiful mountains to the lush, green valleys. A mere trickle of water from a spring soon becomes a branch, stream, and rushing river in no time at all.

The world is some kind of ecosystem. How could something so perfect just evolve? No chance!!! The beauty and balance of nature is beyond our human comprehension and understanding. A greater power must be responsible for such perfection. The human body itself is too intricate in its design to have merely evolved from a tadpole.

There are many theories on the creation of the world and mankind. Who knows exactly how God created everything. God's ways are higher than our ways. We are not necessarily supposed to understand it, but to accept it with simple faith. Thank you Lord for all that you have so richly blessed us with. May we always respect and preserve your precious gift.

"For by Him all things were created: Things in heaven and on earth, visible and invisible, Whether thrones or powers or rulers or authorities: All things were created by Him and for Him." Colossians 1:16

Grandpa and Grandma Naumann with a
mess of fish back in the 50's.

Tradition

We all have been raised somewhere in "God's Country". In my home state of North Carolina, you will still hear some good 'ol boys refer to this region as "God's Country". It is a prideful phrase commonly used to describe many beautiful places around the United States. There is nothing wrong with being so proud of your "stomping grounds". God created it all!

I was fortunate to have been raised in a family that loved the outdoors. Both of my grandfathers were avid hunters and fishermen. One of my grandmothers even enjoyed fishing and deer hunting! I've got the old Winchester Model 94 that she carried in the woods. I will always be grateful to my dad for taking me fishing at an early age. I must have been "knee-high to a duck" the first time he took me. The desire to be in the outdoors has burned in me ever since.

I was always taught to appreciate and respect wildlife and their habitat. These traditions are passed down from generation to generation. I anxiously await the day when I can take my children fishing or hunting. It is our responsibility to teach our children and grandchildren what "God's Country" truly means. God has so much to teach us all through His Creation.

"Before the mountains were born, You brought forth the earth and the world, from everlasting to everlasting You are God." Psalm 90:2

Amazin' Grace

God created man for a far greater purpose than to just "tend the garden". He created us in His own image, in His own likeness. The purpose was to have a special relationship with us. He only asked Adam and Eve not to eat of the fruit from only one tree. With all that God had given them you would think they could have held off on the forbidden fruit. No chance!

We are like cattle in a fenced pasture, always curious about the grass on the other side of the fence. Adam and Eve blew it, and so have we ever since. They had it all. Adam probably was the first to coin the phrase, "This is God's Country", when referring to the Garden of Eden. God desires for us to love and honor Him through obedience. How can we atone for our disobedience and sin?

"For all have sinned and fallen short of the glory of God." (Romans 3:23). How do we come back to a right relationship with a Holy God? A penalty must be paid. Our sin was a debt we could never repay. That is why God sent His only Son Jesus Christ to die for us.

It is the saving grace of Jesus that enables us to fully appreciate all that God has created from the beginning. Whether I'm sitting in a tree stand or wading a trout stream, I thank the Lord for all His blessings. Many of us take for granted being able to climb a tree or wade a stream.

How can we forget the words in the classic hymn, "Amazing grace, how sweet the sound, that saved a wretch like me. I once was lost but now I'm found, was blind, but now I see." Thank God everyday for His amazin' grace.

Deer Stand Devotions

It is so difficult for us to hear God speaking to our hearts. I believe we are just too busy to listen. Everyone has their own daily routine. We work, eat, and sleep most of the time in a 24-hour day. Time management becomes our focus. Where did all the time go? The last I checked, there is the same number of hours in a day now as there was in 1940.

It wasn't too long ago that God, family, and the front porch swing were a way of life for most. There is so much available now to keep us busy and entertained. We panic if we lose the remote control to the TV! Our response is always, "I don't have time!" I am reminded of that the moment I climb up in a deer stand. It is as if God says, "It's about time you slowed down enough so I could talk to you." What a great opportunity to spend intimate time with our Savior and Lord.

I do pray on the way from the truck to my stand that something doesn't get me in the dark. You know what I'm talking about. It's an hour before daybreak. You're walking up a hollow of dense hardwoods and a bobcat cries out nearby. You wet your pants and start praying, "Lord, just get me up in that deer stand!" We've all been there. It's part of the excitement and thrill of the hunt.

As the sun slowly breaks the tree line, it is as if God turned on a light switch. The once quiet forest comes alive. Birds begin singing, squirrels scratch around, and a mosquito is buzzing in your ear. The beauty and serenity of the moment humble me. God is never more real to me that at that time.

Regardless of the outcome of the hunt, spend some time with the Lord in prayer. Tell Him what's on your heart and mind. Whatever you might be doing in the outdoors, use the time to draw close to God.

Life gets real quiet when you sit in a deerstand. You're just a little closer to God when you're 15 feet off the ground.

The Anchor Holds

I have been a fisherman since I was in the womb or sometime soon after. My grandparents owned a trailer on a small lake outside Jackson, Michigan. It was their weekend getaway. It was also a family tradition to vacation there on the 4th of July. As a young boy, I lived for the day I could take out the 'ol rowboat by myself to fish. One of the best-known "honey holes" was on the other side of the lake and could only be fished by boat.

The day finally came when I was 8 years old. My Granddad told me I would need oars, a cushion, lifejacket, and an anchor. I gathered all my fishing tackle, loaded up, and rowed all the way across the lake without one thing - the anchor! You know the slightest wind will cause a boat to drift. A storm moved in quickly and I had no anchor. I was scared to death as I fought the wind. Thankfully, I was able to get back to shore safely.

I think about that fearful day when I go through troubled time in life. When the storms of life rage against you, did you forget the anchor? Jesus Christ is our anchor in a life that gets pretty rough at times. We often turn to other things for comfort when facing a trial. We search for solutions and answers.

It is important for us to realize that it is God that brings peace in the midst of the storm. It is through faith in Him that we know the anchor holds.

The ocean can be a dangerous place with no anchor, but I was blessed to catch a near state record Red Drum off St. Simons Island, Georgia.

I slowly work my way downstream on the Nantahala River in the NC Mountains.

River Runs Through It

In the blockbuster movie, A River Runs Through It, Robert Redford's character grew up with a passion for fly fishing for trout. What awesome scenery in that flick! There's nothing like slipping on the waders, putting on the felt-bottom boots, and wading a pristine trout stream.

I attended Mars Hill University in the Appalachian Mountains of western North Carolina. The area lays claim to some of the best trout water in the country. One of my personal favorites is the Nantahala River near the NC/Tennessee line. Many locals will argue that the surrounding area truly is "God's Country".

I'll never forget one foggy morning when I stepped in the river and a bobcat was watching me from the bank on the other side. I thanked the Lord instantly for such an awesome sight. The bobcat disappeared in the laurel bushes and I soon caught a nice rainbow. I proceeded to work downstream from hole to hole. Now some folks prefer to fish upstream, but it is usually easier to go with the flow than to fight the current in big water like the Nantahala.

In the same way, we tend to fight the swift current in our lives. We live the way we want, do what we want, when we want to. The happiness that we experience doing it "our way" is only temporary when compared to the joy found in doing God's will.

God has a perfect plan for our lives. It is up to us to yield to His direction for our lives. I am reminded of the classic hymn. "Trust and obey, for there's no other way…" It's a whole lot easier to fish downstream. Try is sometime.

Hog Wild!

Have you ever been so afraid that you literally ask God to deliver you? It sounds funny, but I've done so on many occasions. During my freshman year in college, I hunted and fished more than I ever studied. One of my favorite hunting spots was Flattop Mountain in Yancey County. You talk about beautiful country! Back in those days, I often hunted the mountains by myself. Not the wisest thing to do.

I was bow hunting miles from nowhere late one evening. As I slipped along a logging road, I could hear something rustling the leaves in the hollow above me. It sounded like several deer scratching the forest floor in search of acorns. The stalk was on. I went into "stealth" mode! The sounds led me into a laurel thicket. On my all fours, I inched closer to the persistent sounds.

As the source of the sound became visible, all I saw were a bunch of black-haired Russian Boar. My heart sank as I searched for a nearby tree to climb. There was no tree around that would hold up my 240 lb. self. I was "as nervous as a cat on a rotten limb". I actually closed my eyes and prayed, "Lord, please help me. I'll never eat bacon or barbecue again." Boy, have I broken that promise since that day.

We can really pray when we are in trouble, can't we? It is so easy not to call upon God when times are good and all is right with the world.

Well, the Lord heard my plea as I was able to slowly crawl away undetected. Call upon the Lord in all things, before they've gone "hog wild".

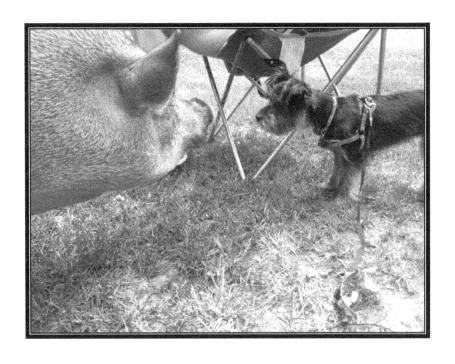

Showdown! Our family dog Marley comes face to face to with our pet hog Olive.

Living In A Shell

While flounder fishing in a tidewater creek in South Carolina, I noticed an abundance of hermit crabs in the shallow water. I was busy laying out the flounder by jigging a white split-tail grub. I was equipped with a light-action spinning rod and 6 lb. test line. The flounder were in 4 ft. of water feeding on minnows as the tide fell early in the morning.

I had already caught and released three fish over 14 inches when I hooked the granddaddy of the flounder family. The fish led me up and down the creek. The huge fish looked to be about 2 ft. long as it pulled line from my reel. When a flounder turns its body sideways, you're in for a real fight. It would have been the biggest flounder I've ever caught. The key words being "would have been" as the fish broke my line. Defeated, I walked to the bank.

Again, I noticed those hermit crabs crawling all over the sandy bottom. I thought I would take a couple with me to show to my one-year old son. Every time you pick the shell up, the crab retreats out of sight. Hidden deep within the shell, the hermit crab is safe from predators. I couldn't help but feel sorry for the little fellows. They have to lug that shell with them wherever they go.

How much are we like the hermit crab? We too spend much of our lives in a shell. We feel vulnerable and at risk in many areas of our lives. We would rather withdraw into our shell than risk being hurt or wounded. How much do we miss out on in life by living in a shell? We are unable to experience all that God has for us if we shelter ourselves. We do the same in relationships with others. As soon as we feel threatened, we pull back and hide.

We all have a shell of some kind. Sure they can be protective and even beautiful on the outside; but, they are also heavy and cumbersome. We have to haul that thing around as a defense mechanism. We can receive so much from God and others if we just lose the shell! Jesus Christ bore our sin and shame on the cross so that we wouldn't have to carry that 'ol shell around anymore.

Soar Like An Eagle

The American Bald Eagle symbolizes freedom of the United States. This majestic bird represents life, liberty, and the pursuit of something better. I have seen only two Bald Eagles in the wild. On the way to deer hunt one afternoon, I saw an eagle soaring high above a mountain peak. I almost wrecked my truck as I watched bewildered. Thank you Lord for such an awesome sight!

The second sighting took place in Michigan. I was perch fishing when I saw a Bald Eagle gracefully fly across the water with a fish in its talons. It landed in the top of a tree to enjoy his catch. I almost fell out of the boat as I witnessed the event. I think the eagle caught more fish than I did that day.

The experience made me think of Isaiah 40:31: *"...but those who hope in the Lord will renew their strength. They will soar on wings like eagles; they will run and not grow weary, they will walk and not be faint."* You can understand why Isaiah chose the eagle to make a point. An eagle soars higher than all other species of bird. While all the other fowl live close to the ground, the eagle flies high atop the food chain. The eagle's view is better than any bird as it hovers effortlessly over the ground below.

God is telling us in His Word to soar like an eagle. As His children, we are to live high above the world's standards. We are not here to lead mediocre lives; rather, we can fly high like the eagle.

Eagle Country - Spectacular view from the Naumann Family Cabin on the St. Mary's River near Sault Ste. Marie, Michigan.

Strength In Numbers

There are very few animals that inhabit the earth that are loners. I'm sure you could come up with a few. However, many species are group or family oriented. You often see a herd of deer, a flock of turkeys, or a covey of quail. There were many hunting trips that I wanted to see one deer, let alone a herd!

Take time to study the behavior of any animal. They are very relational with their own kind. Mothers tend to their offspring. Young animals joyfully play together. I love to watch squirrels chase each other up and down an oak tree or see fawns running in circles in an open field.

When it comes to survival, animals find solace and strength in numbers. A covey of quail will huddle close together when a predator is nearby. If you mess with one hornet, you mess with the whole hive! God created us in the same way. We too are creatures that need family and fellowship.

It is not meant for us to go it alone in life. For that reason, it is very important for us to be a part of a church fellowship.

Regardless of the denomination, to be close to the Body of Christ.

Read John 15. A branch apart from the vine cannot bear fruit. This is a fundamental principle in Gardening 101 and in life. Open your heart to others and be accountable. It is then that you will find strength in numbers.

Below The Surface

I Samuel 16:7 says, *"Man looks at the outward appearance, but the Lord looks at the heart."* My wife and I went on a cruise for our honeymoon to several islands in the Caribbean. On Barbados, we had the opportunity to do some snorkeling. Now, for the avid outdoorsman, anything to do with animals or fish is worth while.

Have you noticed that when you look at the surface of the ocean, all you see is waves, foam, and a little seaweed? It is when we peer below the surface that we gain a completely new perspective. Magnificently colored fish swim peacefully in and around the jagged coral reef. It's as if you were actually inside a well-decorated fish bowl!

There was more variety in sea creatures than people at an airport. You would never know how spectacular the ocean is by merely looking at the surface. God didn't play around when He created the ocean! I wonder sometimes what He thought of the movie Jaws? It sure makes me think twice about body surfing.

How often do we form our opinion about things based on what we see? All the time…it is our nature. It can be especially dangerous in our relationships with others. We cast judgment upon people with little knowledge of who they really are.

Aren't you glad that God didn't take a long look at you and say, "By the looks of this one, he's not worth a plug nickel." Rather, God looks beyond our appearance to our soul, the very core of our existence, and sees us for who we are. Try a little snorkeling, get below the surface, and find what is genuine and real in life and others.

*It always felt good to get back to my old Ford
pickup when I had temporarily lost my way.*

Where's The Truck?

Have you ever been lost in the woods? Man, I've been lost in the dark and the light! It's not difficult to lose your bearings without a compass, landmarks, and reflective tape. I forgot...we've got GPS now too.

Most of my early hunting experience took place in the rugged mountains of North Carolina. You hike a few miles in, cross over a few ridges and hollows, and you'll wish you had a flare gun.

I had been tracking some fresh deer tracks that led me astray one time. No sidewalks or street signs. No gas stations or payphones to ask for directions. I'm normally good at marking where I have been, but my mind was focused entirely on the hunt. I soon realized it was approaching nightfall and I needed to find the truck. I kept telling myself, the truck should be directly over the next ridge. No chance!

Being completely lost is a frightening experience. It is the same feeling you get separated from your folks in a huge department store...lost! We've all been there one time or another. In the same way, we are lost in this world without

God. We try to find our way through life with everything else but God. With no direction, we wander aimlessly from person to person and place to place.

We can find real comfort in Proverbs 3:5-6: "*Trust in the Lord with all your heart and lean not on your own understanding, but in all your ways acknowledge Him, and He will direct your path.*" Look it up again whenever you ask yourself, "Where's the truck?"

The Lord is my Shepherd

"The Lord is my shepherd,

I shall not be in want.

He makes me lie down in green pastures,

He leads me beside quiet waters,

He restores my soul.

He guides me in paths of righteousness

For His Name's sake.

Even though I walk through

The valley of the shadow of death,

I will fear not evil,

For you are with me;

Your rod and your staff,

They comfort me."

Psalm 23:1-4

My beautiful daughter Tatum protects and cares for her horse Willow like a shepherd tends a flock of sheep.

Seasick In South Myrtle

Seasickness. Have you ever been there, done that? Unfortunately, I must raise my hand. I have suffered knee injuries that paled in comparison to being seasick.

It was my first deep-sea fishing trip. A friend and his father had booked an all day trip on a "party" boat out of South Myrtle Beach, South Carolina. I would soon find out the trip was no party.

Our destination was the Gulf Stream to fish for grouper and red snapper. Having never been out on the open sea in a boat, my friend recommended I take some of those pills to keep you from getting sick. I pridefully said, "No thank you, I'll be fine." Famous last words of a fool.

Why do we men have such big egos? The boat was no more than a mile from the marina, and I was giving it the 'ol heave ho. To make matters worse, the ocean was rough and waves were crashing over the bow of the boat. Everyone was below the deck except me, and another prideful guy with the same problem.

I prayed that the Lord would calm the sea just as He did on Galilee. I finally understood how Gregory Peck must have felt strapped to the back of that white whale. I continued to pray, "Lord, get me to the nearest piece of dry land, do not pass go, do not collect $200." I never wet a line that day but did live to tell about it!

So often we depend on God to bail us out and we blame Him for our circumstances. Remember that He blessed us with a keen mind and spirit to make good decisions. God is working behind the scenes without us knowing it.

I am always reminded of the man that was caught in a great flood. As the floodwaters rose, he stood atop the chimney of his home. He prayed hard for God to deliver him from peril. A boat came by soon after and urged him to get in. The man said, "No thank you, God will deliver me." A second boat came by and his response was the same. With the water about to overtake him, a helicopter hovered overhead. The rescue team lowered a ladder and with a megaphone said, "Sir, climb up the ladder, you don't have much time!" Again the man responded, "My God will deliver me!" The man perished in the flood soon after. When he stood before God in Heaven, he asked, "Lord, I had faith that you would deliver me from the great flood. Why didn't you?" God answered, "I sent you two boats and a helicopter!"

Remember that God often works through the lives of people to accomplish His purpose. By the way, the next time I went deep-sea fishing…I took those pills.

Lost At Sea

Alright, it really wasn't at "sea" I was lost on a year ago. It sounded good for the title. It was Fontana Lake in the North Carolina Mountains. The lake is quite remote, absent of any residential or commercial development. You can just about get lost on that lake in broad daylight let alone at night.

Some friends and I were smallmouth bass fishing on a warm spring evening. We had caught several nice fish when a dense fog set in on the lake. I'd never seen anything like it in all my days. You literally couldn't see your hand in front of your face! We had our running lights on and hollered for help to no avail. We had to drop anchor to keep from drifting into the bank. My friend's father was in another boat further down the lake. It was hours until we heard a faint voice, "Boys, where are you?"

My buddy immediately recognized his father's voice. "Daddy!" he yelled back. Soon after, we were found and all made it home.

Did you know that a flock of sheep recognizes only the voice of their shepherd? That's the truth. God the Father is our Shepherd; and, we are His sheep.

He calls us with a still, small voice that only we can hear. He seeks to love and tend to us. When we are lost, He leads us home. Respond to the Lord when He calls you by name. Stop and listen. You'll know His voice.

*This pic was taken before nightfall as the fog started to set in
on Fontana Lake in Bryson City, NC. We were lost
an hour later!*

You never know what you might find on a sandy road in the South Carolina Lowcountry.

Rattlesnake In The Road

While deer hunting in the low country of South Carolina, I came across a huge snake in the middle of a dirt road. I stopped the truck, got out, and approached the snake like I was a highway patrolman. It didn't take too long for me to realize it was a big 'ol rattlesnake. It wasn't rattling for the fun of it either.

You know the devil sits coiled up, ready to strike at us. "Be self-controlled and alert. Your enemy the devil prowls around like a roaring lion looking for someone to devour." 1 Peter 5:8.

We sometimes fall into temptation because of our own selfish curiosity and desire. Warning signs like the "rattle" are often disregarded. It's no wonder sin bites us on the ankle. The instant I heard that rattlesnake, I set a high-jump world record when I cleared the tailgate of my truck!

Pray for wisdom and discernment that we may see the devil all coiled up and ready to strike. You may think twice about identifying what lies ahead in the middle of the road. It could be a rattlesnake.

Rusty anxiously awaits my arrival home from school. He would always watch me come down the drive.

Man's Best Friend

Dogs have long been referred to as "man's best friend". How many of us had a dog as a childhood pet? I'm not talking about cats now, just good 'ol dawgs!

I got my first dog at the age of 10. He was the pick of the litter, a mixed breed of Golden Lab and Brittany Spaniel. His name was Rusty. Rusty was everything to everybody... a friend, guardian, and a pretty good bird-dog too. We put up many a covey of quail together. Back at the house, he would tree a squirrel or raccoon in a minute.

Rusty and I shared some special times together. Through my laughter and my tears, he was always there, as warm and faithful as the sunrise in the morning. Rusty passed away at the age of 14. I couldn't help but cry and grieve over the loss of such a wonderful companion.

You know God too wants to be "man's best friend". He loves us unconditionally and waits up for us when we stray away. I'll never forget Rusty anxiously looking out the window as the car rolled into the drive.

God feels much the same when we come home to Him. He wants to be man's best friend. If dogs do go to Heaven, it was Rusty's loyalty that got him there.

Our log cabin atop a mountain in Burke County, NC
is a place of serenity.

No Place Like Home

It is a fact that the vast majority of hunters are men. With that said, listen up men! As the North Carolina deer season drew to a close, I grew anxious to hunt just a few more times.

I managed to sneak off on a Saturday morning to my "honey hole" on a private farm close to home. The temperature was freezing and rainy. It wasn't long before I was ready to head for the house. The deer probably watched me shiver in the stand and thought, "This guy is either dedicated or stupid!" A little of both I reckon. Maybe I deserved a little punishment for not staying home that morning.

My wife and boy wanted me to stay home with many things to do and fun to have. I hunted anyway and didn't see a cotton pickin' thing. Not even a squirrel, let alone a deer. God humbles us to show us what our priorities are and what they should be. The great Vince Lombardi once said that his loyalty was to "God, family, and the Green Bay Packers." Where do we put our hobbies and interests in our list of priorities? I am as passionate as anyone when it comes to the outdoors, but fail to show such passion consistently for the Lord and my loved ones.

Sometimes it takes a cold, miserable experience to help us realize that there is no place like home. Thank you God for showing us what is truly important in life. Our relationships with God and family are far more important than hanging an 8 pointer on the wall. I guess I'll just have to ask my wife to go hunting with me next time. Just kidding Lord.

While it was only a mount of a Brown Bear,

my youngest son Tanner was not so sure.

Lions, Tigers, and Bears

In the southeastern region of God's Country, there is an abundance of wildlife including deer, bear, turkey, and many other species. What you won't see much of are mountain lions, although they do inhabit the south.

The cats are more commonly referred to as a cougar, panther, or puma. A lion in the south is more of a myth than a reality as they are quite rare.

I hunted often with a friend at a hunt club in the Low country of South Carolina. He had never hunted much before and gleamed with excitement and anticipation of the hunt. On one occasion, I gave him my old Winchester Model 94 30.30 and set him on the ground on the edge of a cut cornfield.

When we met back at the cabin after the hunt, his face was as "white as a sheet". He said he saw a bobcat and it scared him to death. I laughed and explained to him that a bobcat is harmless. Interested in his encounter, I probed further and asked, "Did it have pretty coat with black spots?" "No, it was solid, grayish-brown in color," he exclaimed.

At this point, I thought that his inexperience in the field was the reason for the false identification. I then asked, "Did the cat have a bobbed tail?" He then responded, "No, it had a body about 4 feet long with a tail 2-3 feet long!" I knew in an instant that what he had seen was no bobcat or housecat. The mountain lion had come within 10 yards of him. The state DNR confirmed there were some pumas in the area.

You know, the devil lurks about much like that mountain lion. My friend was unsure exactly what kind of animal it was. As Christians, it is important for us to know who the enemy is to keep from being attacked. Stay close to the Lord and His Word to discern who the enemy is. Don't be caught off guard!

Sitting in a deerstand with my son Tucker

is what being a father is all about.

In His Sights

Hunting equipment has come a long way with the technological advancements made over the last several years. There seems to be a gadget that serves any purpose you can think of, from bow quivers to gun scopes. The new in-line muzzleloaders have an effective range that is comparable to many rifles. I'm still using the 'ol 50 caliber hammerlock if you're wondering. Missed a deer this past season with it too!

The quality of hunting optics and scopes on the market is unbelievable. You can buy a riflescope now that gathers so much light, you can practically hunt at night if it were legal. I hope you're not one of those that do anyway! We have long referred to putting a scope on an animal as having the animal "in your sights".

Think about the times you've seen a buck come into view. You ease your rifle up, look through the scope or open sights, steady the crosshairs on the buck, and say to yourself, "I've got him in my sights…boom!"

You know God hunts for man in the same way. He is intently glassing the world searching for you and I to have a personal relationship with Him. Jesus Christ even called his disciples to be "fishers of men". It is important to remember that as God looks for us and calls us by name. We need to respond to Him in faith.

Through some of the most troubled times of my life, I know that God kept a watchful eye on me. Do you know God personally and intimately? If so, you have the blessed assurance that you will always be "in His sights".

Peace on McAlpine Creek

Growing up in Charlotte, North Carolina was a wonderful experience. We lived in a development that, in the 80's, was on the border of town and country. Oh how the South Charlotte area has changed!

Our family would travel on Hwy 51 from Pineville to Matthews on an old two-lane road with a 55 mph speed limit. You can't drive 100 yards anymore without having to stop for something. No wonder I live in Union County now. I'll probably be at the beach by the time the growth slows down.

Our property adjoined hundreds of acres of undeveloped woods and wetlands. McAlpine Creek, about 10 to 20 feet wide, gracefully meandered behind our house. There was a well-beaten path through the hardwoods that led to the creek. McAlpine Creek was home to many species of fish including bass, bream, catfish, and an occasional crappie.

When the Japanese beetles would invade Charlotte in the summer, I would gather dozens at a time and put them into a cricket keeper. I'd grab my trusty Zebco 202 fishing rod, beetles, and dog Rusty and head out. Rusty, my faithful companion, would watch anxiously from the bank, as I would catch fish by the tubful. Never was a beetle set free, unfortunately. If records were kept, I'll bet my eyeteeth that I've caught more fish out of McAlpine Creek that anyone in Mecklenburg County.

Never did I keep a fish that I caught from that creek. It was simply a safe haven for a young boy with a lot of energy. As I fished, I would whistle, "Bob white, bob white", and a quail would always respond in kind. Thinking it was always the same bobwhite quail; I named him "Charlie". Charlie would always answer my call on McAlpine Creek.

With the increasing pressures of school and adolescence, when on the creek, I found refuge between its banks and peace in its waters. Find the McAlpine Creek in your life and talk to God there.

In Matthew 11:28, Jesus says, *"Come to me, all who are weary and burdened, and I will give you rest."* I am reminded of those days on the creek when I hear the precious words in an old childhood song, "I've got peace like a river, I've got peace like a river, I've got peace like a river in my soul."

That is me as a young boy in the distance fishing my honeyhole on McAlpine Creek in Charlotte, NC.

In His Hand

"In His hand are the depths of the earth,

and the mountain peaks belong to Him.

The sea is His, for He made it,

and His hands formed the dry land.

Come let us bow down in worship,

let us kneel before the Lord our Maker;

For He is our God

and we are the people of His pasture,

the flock under His care."

Psalm 95:4-7

Time For Turkey

The alarm clock is blaring and is real close to getting blown up with my 12 gauge. Shotgun at four o'clock in the morning. Time to rise and shine for the opening day of turkey season.

Just for a brief moment you lay there questioning your mental stability by getting up at that time of day. You know it's early when you say a morning prayer and realize that the Lord isn't even up yet! Why do we torture ourselves purposefully? The answer is simple…for the love of the game. It is the thrill of the hunt that drives us to extreme measures.

I'll never forget the year that I woke up late on opening day of turkey season in Madison County, North Carolina. I was so anxious to get to the woods before daylight that I put the "pedal to the metal". Unfortunately, a state trooper pulled me over doing 81 in a 55 mph zone. As the trooper approached the side of my truck, there I sat in full camo, owl hooter around my neck, and shotgun in the passenger's seat.

He said, "Boy, where you goin' in such a hurry this mornin'?" I quickly responded, "I'm sorry officer but I was runnin' late for my turkey hunt!"

I believe the trooper felt a little sorry for me that spring morning, but not enough to keep from giving me my first ticket at the age of 19.

Despite the mishap, I was still on a mission. To hear the bone-chilling gobble of a wild turkey amidst the tall hardwoods is an invigorating experience. The adrenaline rush is unbelievable! Suddenly, 4:00 AM doesn't seem all that early.

I may have to join a support group like "Hunters Anonymous" for help. I can see it now, sitting in front of a bunch of guys in camo as I emotionally mutter, "My name is Tom…I'm an obsessed hunter."

How much greater is our passion for God? It was He that gave His very best to us in the person of His Son, Jesus Christ. Are we as fired up about going to church as we are the woods? As hunters, we equip ourselves with the best gun, gadgets, and gear that money can buy. We get up at "dark thirty" to hit the woods yet we struggle to get to church by 9:30 in the morning.

Just as the challenge of the hunt requires our very best, God requires the same in our relationship with Him. May we seek Him with the same passion and zeal we show for the outdoors.

Dad and I fishing for crappie at Lone Mtn. Lake

in the mountains of Tennessee.

The One That Got Away

Anglers have forever told their stories about "the one that got away", or in my case, the "many" that got away. I am haunted to this day by the memory of the brook trout that got away in a small stream in the mountains of North Carolina.

One of my favorite honey holes was Upper Bowlens Creek near Mount Mitchell. At the time, this small creek offered some of the best brook trout fishing in the state.

Fly fishing with a Tellico nymph, I caught and released about 20 fish as I worked my way downstream. Brook trout, commonly referred to as "specks" by locals, don't grow much larger that the length of your hand. As a rule of thumb in those parts, a speck over 12 inches is a true wall hanger.

As I approached the largest hole in that stretch of water, I let the current carry my nymph along a steep bank and under a large boulder. I quickly noticed that the fly had come to an abrupt halt so I gave a little jerk as I thought I was hung up. As I pulled firmly to free up the nymph, out rolled the biggest, most beautiful, blood-red brook trout you have ever seen.

With God as my witness on the bank, the fish was a foot long if it was an inch! As a matter of fact, it already had a wood plaque attached to it and a brass plate engraved with my name…not so fast Tom. Before I could land the trophy, it threw that fly right back in my face. Prozac anyone? Depression set in real quick as I headed straight for the truck.

Did you know that God in Heaven grieves over people who are lost and wandering without purpose? He "fishes for men" through His Son Jesus and doesn't like to go home "skunked". His desire is to have a personal relationship with you and me.

If you've never experienced salvation, simply ask Jesus Christ to come into your heart and life as your Savior and Lord. May God never have to refer to you as "the one that go away."

Major In Men, Minor In Fish

It's no wonder Jesus used parables and stories to make a point. He spoke in terms that were relevant to the people around Him. Many of His parables had something to do with the outdoors whether it be fishing or planting. Why? Because that's what most of the folks could relate to, just as we do today.

Read Matthew 4:18-20. Jesus met Simon Peter and Andrew while they were fishing. The brothers were probably members of the Galilee Chapter of Bassmasters. They fished for a living; they were on the tournament trail! Here comes a stranger, Jesus, who says, "Come follow me, and I will make you fishers of men."

How they responded to His call makes all the difference. They didn't say, "Let us think about it a few days" or "Let me talk it over with my wife and I'll get back to ya." In absolute faith, the Bible says, "At once they dropped their nets and followed Him!"

Now I have fished all my life and I don't plan on quitting anytime soon, but are we as diligent in sharing our faith with others as we are catching fish? It doesn't necessarily mean you have to sell your tackle and boat (Unless you value your bass boat more that your wife!).

God wants us to focus on eternal things. A friend coming to know Christ personally and going to Heaven is a whole lot more important than the 10 lb. largemouth bass you want to hang on the wall. Think about switching your major to "men", and minor in "fish".

It's not the Sea of Galilee, but a beautiful campsite on Fontana Lake. How I love to camp and fish for Walleye in the NC Mountains.

In 1989, I took my sweet Mamaw Black and Uncle Grant to visit her sister, Aunt Tishie at the head of Mudlick Holler in Bell County, KY.

The Great Kentucky Flood

In the mountains of Southeastern Kentucky, there lies the sleepy little town of Pineville. Pineville, the county seat for Bell County, was the home place of my mother's family. We often took family trips to there to visit my great grandparents, Mamaw and Papaw Black.

Mamaw and Papaw loved to fish together in the TVA rivers and lakes that made up the region. As a young boy, I could see Jesus Christ glorified through their lives. They were simple folks with a simple faith, lacking nothing in terms of necessity.

Mamaw is the reason to this day that when asked what my favorite food is, I proudly exclaim, "Biscuits and gravy"! She make the best milk gravy known to man in that 'ol black skillet. Her southern-fried chicken wasn't too bad either.

In 1977, as massive flood hit Pineville and practically destroyed the whole town. The town was surrounded on all sides by ridges and the river passed through it. With days of torrent rainfall, the floodwaters engulfed the entire town.

When the water receded, Mamaw and Papaw returned home to survey the damage. Mud and silt had destroyed everything in sight. Upon further investigation, they noticed the family Bible sitting on the coffee table in its usual place. I can remember seeing that Bible there my whole life.

The Bible was unharmed by the flood! There wasn't a watermark on a single page! It sounds unbelievable, but it couldn't be any further from the truth. God had protected the one thing that was most precious to them.

Mamaw and Papaw knew the power of the Word. While they lost furniture, clothes, and memorable pictures, their Bible was kept safe from the flooding water.

No matter what storms of life you face, God's Word will always remain the same. Its power and presence in our lives will forever be unchanged.

Trail of Tears

Native Americans hold a special place in the history of the United States. You talk about "God's Country", nobody appreciated it more than those who came before us. They were quite the outdoorsmen, proficient in hunting, trapping, and fishing. Imagine a time when God's Creation was unspoiled by modern civilization.

From my mother's side of the family in the mountains of Southeastern Kentucky, I am proud to carry Cherokee blood. My Mamaw Black often bragged on my jet-black hair, a trait inherited from our Cherokee ancestors. "Hair as black as coal," she would claim. It has long been a living reminder of the Cherokee history of tradition and tragedy. The Cherokee people were forced to move from their native land in what was known as the "Trail of Tears".

I had the privilege of working closely with the Cherokee as an insurance agent in the early 90's. It was my first job out of college. The agency served the Eastern Band of the Cherokee Indians in the Great Smokey Mountains of North Carolina.

If you were to look in the file cabinet at the office, you would find many last names derived from the outdoors: Running Deer, Standing Deer, Climbing Bear, Owl, Crow, Feather, Cucumber, and the list goes on. "Yes Mr. Running Deer, your policy will be effective tomorrow" was a common occurrence!

Every once in a while, one of the elder Cherokee would come to the office and couldn't speak a word of English. They would just stare at me. I'll never forget the burley fellow from the Owl family that paid his insurance premiums with the money he made by hunting ginseng. There were many stories I could tell about my experience with these people.

What can we learn from our Native American ancestors? Just as they were persecuted years ago, Christians have long suffered in the same way. In a sinful world, it is not always popular to take a stand for Christ. In the midst of darkness, we are called to "let our light shine before men." Government legislation and intervention stifles the values and principles this country was founded on.

No one understands better what the Cherokee Indians endured than Jesus Christ. Take the time to read Luke 23:26-

43. After being beaten and scorned, He carried the cross to another place, a hill called Golgotha.

The road that led to Calvary was a "Trail of Tears" for our Savior and Lord. However, it was in that painful journey and experience that we find forgiveness, hope, and eternal life.

My gray wolf Dakota is ready to pounce
on anything that comes to the front porch.

Crying Wolf

With Cherokee Indian ancestry, I have always been intrigued by Native American symbols such as feathers, cattle skulls, and wolves. They represent an era long forgotten by many.

A few years back, I ran into a fellow that raised wolf hybrids. They were a cross between a Gray Wolf and an Alaskan Malamute. I'm talking about some kind of beautiful now. At the time, I had a coonhound that I eventually gave to a buddy of mine to make room for the wolf.

I purchased that little wolf pup for $500. To go along with the Native American tradition, I named him Dakota. He looked more like a possum when I brought him home because of his grayish-white fur. He was cuter than a "speckled pup in a basket" too. Little did I know what I was getting into!

Dakota had a high percentage of Gray Wolf in his genes. There was very little resemblance of an Alaskan Malamute. He looked exactly like Two Socks, the wolf in the movie, Dances with Wolves. He quickly began to grow in knowledge and stature. I have always learned that wolves are highly intelligent and reclusive animals. Dakota was no exception.

I kept Dakota in a 10' x 10' kennel with an automatic water and feeding trough. His living conditions were as good as mine at the time. I came home from work one afternoon and found him loose outside of the kennel. The enclosure had a top on it and the gate was locked so I was puzzled as to how he pulled a "Houdini" on me. As I looked closely at the chain link fence that surrounded the pen, I noticed that metal ties that fastened the fence to the poles had been untwisted. With the fence just dangling, Dakota was able to squeeze out without any problem.

After repairing the fence, I put Dakota back in the kennel and went in the house. Like a private investigator, I camped out by the window to watch what he was doing. Without delay, that rascal would get those metal ties in his teeth and turn his head like a screwdriver. He untwisted and pulled everyone of those things off! I thought to myself, "I don't have a pet. I've got the devil!" I'd never seen such problem-solving intelligence in a canine.

All kinds of thoughts ran through my head from that day forward. Normal dogs bring rodents to the porch, Dakota was gonna start dragging deer up to the house! As I would sit in the recliner and he would stare at me, I felt I was a hot dog.

I learned something with Dakota. Just as God wonderfully made us, He created animals in the same way. Whether domestic or wild animals, take note of His work. Such beauty does not merely evolve. God created everything you see with meaning and purpose.

"I have fought the good fight, I have finished the race, I have kept the faith". 2 Timothy 4:7

Death Of A Legend

My dad and I watched the Daytona 500 and Michael Waltrip drive to victory lane for the first time. His celebration, however, was dampened somewhat by the news that his car owner, Dale Earnhardt, was in critical condition.

We later would find out that Dale Earnhardt, a racing legend, had died from the injuries suffered when his car hit the wall in the 4th turn of the final lap. Ironically, the final lap of the race was also the final lap of his life. We lost a good man that day.

For those that followed stock car racing closely, you would know that Dale Earnhardt had one passion that rivaled racing...hunting. He purely loved to spend time in the woods when he wasn't on the track. Dale was an accomplished hunter, harvesting many trophy animals over his life. As much as he loved the competition of racing, he longed to just be himself and one with nature.

Our lives are much like the Daytona 500. The green flag drops when we are born and off we go, through our childhood, adolescence, and so on. The race we run is a long, grueling event, requiring a few pit stops along the way. Like a racecar, we get jacked up, change tires, refuel, and get back on the track.

As the race continues, we stumble spiritually by hitting the wall or other cars. We grow so tired and weary that the caution may come out, or a red flag to halt the race. We struggle as we move on, closer to he finish line.

Like the Daytona 500, the race of our life must come to an end. The white flag will come out indicating one lap to go and we take the checkered flag. It is inevitable that the race comes to an end. Take out your Bible and read 2 Timothy 4:6-8. What will you say to the Lord on that day? Keep the faith.

Time is short as evidenced by such a tragic loss. Many of us have lost loved ones along the way. No one knew but God what would happen to Dale Earnhardt that fateful day.

Though we are never promised tomorrow here on earth, we may find eternal security in Jesus Christ. Fight the good fight and keep the faith.

Roles And Responsibilities

Have you ever recognized a need and selfishly responded, "Someone will take care of it." I'm sure there's a few folks that said that their vote didn't matter in an election too.

It is a fact that God created the heavens and the earth. Were there outdoorsmen back in Bible times? Are you kidding? Deer hunters were heading for the woods before Jesus was born.

As outdoorsmen of the present, we have been ordained with the responsibility of conserving our wildlife and their habitats. Who better to answer the call than we who appreciate and enjoy His Creation? How can we help? The purchase of licenses is one way. In addition, help may be given through financial support or volunteer work with any number of wildlife and environmental organizations. It is always a good rule to leave the land in better shape than when you arrived. Pick up trash, plant food plots, maintain wildlife habitat, and so on.

God, thank you for the wonderful gift of Creation you have entrusted to us. May we boldly accept the responsibility and take an active role in preservation and conservation. May we seek you Lord, in all that we see and do in the outdoors.

Acknowledgements

I would like to thank a few folks for their support and assistance in making God's Country a reality.

To my beautiful wife Angie, for her unwavering love and encouragement from the beginning.

To my mother-in-law, Linda Embrey and friend Lindsey Seward, who helped tremendously in the editing and proofreading of the material.

To my huntin' buddies, Pat Kelly, David Beaver, Chip Ferguson, Robby Williams, Garnald Efird, and Lee Wood, for their friendship and prayerful support.

To my brother-in-law and sister, Randy and Chrisy Hatcher, for believing in the vision and me.

To my younger brother Tim, for teaching me the true meaning of dedication and commitment.

To my dear mother, for introducing me to Jesus Christ at a young age. Her unconditional love for God, family, and others is beyond compare.

To the many others in my life who have been a help and encouragement along the way.

"Then God said,

Let us make man in our image,

in our likeness, and let them rule over

the fish of the sea and the birds of the air,

over the livestock, over all the earth,

and over all the creatures that

move along the ground."

God saw all that He had made,

and it was very good."

Genesis 1:26-31